The Penistone Line

Brief Guide and Country Walks

by

Swinburn

D1783952

Site of new Berry Brow Station to be opened 1989

Published by: Kirklees Metropolitan Council
Libraries, Museums & Arts Division
Red Doles Lane
Huddersfield
HD2 1YF

Printed by Regent Print Group Limited · 30 Albert Street · Huddersfield
Telephone: 0484 530789

Introduction

This booklet falls into two parts; first and foremost a passengers' guide to line, past and present; followed by suggestions for a few of the many possible family walks based on the line.

The idea for the booklet came initially from Colin Speakman and Peter Unwin, who did much of the writing. Help and extra material were provided by members of Denby Dale Labour Party and Harold Whitaker, the whole initiative was furthered by the Huddersfield – Penistone – Sheffield Rail Users Association and by Richard Atkinson of Kirklees Technical Services.

All the above would like gratefully to acknowledge the valuable contributions of Jenny Hinchliffe, David Thurlow, Lesley Brook, Richard Brook, Richard Fieldhouse for his railway expertise, the Local History and Archives Department in Huddersfield Library and Isobel Schofield and David Osborne of Kirklees Libraries Museums and Arts for seeing this booklet to publication.

Brockholes Station

In the Beginning...

In his *History of Penistone* (1906), John N. Dransfield quoted the following from a newspaper cutting:

> *"The first sod of the Huddersfield line was cut by Lord Wharncliffe at this end of Wellhouse Cutting on 29th August 1845, and below is a copy of the bill for the lunch of the Directors and friends at the Rose and Crown Inn, Penistone, on that occasion:*

80 gents' lunch at 5s	£20
44 bottles of champagne at 10s	£22
41 bottles of port at 5s 6d	£11 5s 6d
39 bottles of sherry at 5s 6d	£10 14s 6d
3 bottles of soda water at 6d	1s 6d
13 bottles of soda water for band	6s 6d
6 quarts of ale and porter at 6d	3s
39 quarts ale and porter for ringers at 6d	19s 6d
Meat: Mr Miller's men	7s 6d
Broken Glass	4s
Doorkeeper	3s
By cheque to settle £70	£72 17s 6d"

The line opened 1st July 1850.

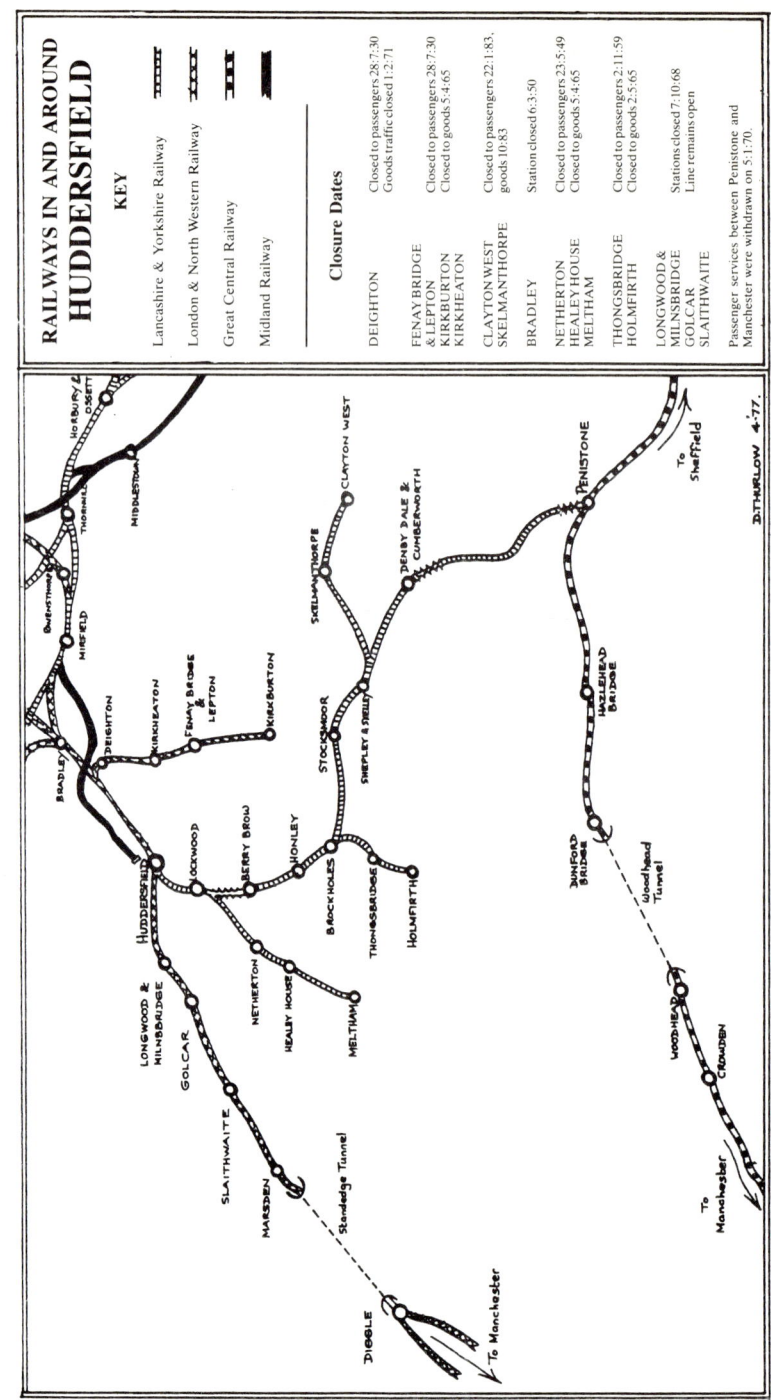

RAILWAYS IN AND AROUND HUDDERSFIELD

KEY

Lancashire & Yorkshire Railway

London & North Western Railway

Great Central Railway

Midland Railway

Closure Dates

DEIGHTON	Closed to passengers 28:7:30 Goods traffic closed 1:2:71
FENAY BRIDGE & LEPTON KIRKBURTON KIRKHEATON	Closed to passengers 28:7:30 Closed to goods 5:4:65
CLAYTON WEST SKELMANTHORPE	Closed to passengers 22:1:83, goods 10:8:3
BRADLEY	Station closed 6:3:50
NETHERTON HEALEY HOUSE MELTHAM	Closed to passengers 23:5:49 Closed to goods 5:4:65
THONGSBRIDGE HOLMFIRTH	Closed to passengers 2:11:59 Closed to goods 2:5:65
LONGWOOD & MILNSBRIDGE GOLCAR SLAITHWAITE	Stations closed 7:10:68 Line remains open

Passenger services between Penistone and
Manchester were withdrawn on 5:1:70.

D.THURLOW 4-'77.

2

Past and Present

On 30th June 1845 Royal Assent was given to an Act that permitted the building of a railway line south from Huddersfield to link up with the newly constructed Sheffield and Manchester Railway at Penistone. The railway boom was underway and local people wanted to link Huddersfield with the rapidly expanding system. The town had no rail services at that time with the nearest station being at Cooper Bridge. The line should have been completed for the end of 1847, however the first trains did not run until 1st July 1850 by which time the route had become a part of the Lancashire and Yorkshire Railway.

At thirteen and a half miles long the line boasts four impressive viaducts and six tunnels. It was built at great expense and with the loss of seven lives. From the very beginning the line had its share of problems... at 8.00 a.m. on the opening day a special train set off to Chatsworth. Dampness on the rails in Thurstonland tunnel brought the struggling engine to a halt. Some of the rear coaches were unhooked so that the front portion of the train could proceed to Penistone whence the engine returned to Thurstonland to collect the unfortunate passengers left behind in the tunnel.

It is no longer possible to travel to Marylebone aboard the South Yorkshireman from Huddersfield, and the old Grand Central line from Manchester to Sheffield has gone. However the line that runs south from Huddersfield to Penistone, Barnsley and Sheffield still has much to offer today's travellers – and much untapped potential.

LANCASHIRE & YORKSHIRE RAILWAY PUBLIC NOTICE

ALL PERSONS ARE HEREBY WARNED NOT TO TRESPASS ON THIS RAILWAY OR ON ANY STATION OR OTHER WORKS LANDS OR PROPERTY OF THE LANCᵉ & YORKᵉ RAILWAY Co. EVERY PERSON SO TRESPASSING AFTER THIS WARNING WILL BE PROSECUTED AND WILL BE LIABLE UNDER SECTION 36 OF THE LANCᵉ & YORKᵉ RAILWAY ACT 1884 TO A PENALTY NOT EXCEEDING FORTY SHILLINGS

BY ORDER

St. George's Square and Station, Huddersfield

*Coats of Arms carved in stone on the facade of Huddersfield station.
The LYR Arms appear to the left of the main entrance and
the HMRC Arms appear to the right of the main entrance.*

4

Huddersfield

The station at Huddersfield is architecturally one of the finest in the country, being a splendid example from the nineteenth century. The central block with its eight Corinthian columns was once a hotel. The two smaller buildings fronted by four columns each, balancing the structure at either end of the station, were originally booking offices for the Lancashire and Yorkshire and the London and North Western railway companies. The foundation stone was laid on 9th October 1846 by Earl Fitzwilliam and was celebrated by a public holiday in the town. The station was completed at a cost of just over £20,000 in 1850.

The station leads directly out onto the grandly spacious St George's Square, the building of which was stimulated by the new railway and is to be restored to some of its former glories in the 1990's. On the left is the George Hotel which was built to replace the George Inn in 1850. The George Inn was removed to improve access to the station and re-erected in St Peter's Street. Facing the station are the Lion Buildings built between 1852 and 1854, crowned with a large statue of a lion and, on the right, the notable Britannia Buildings, completed in 1859, now houses the Yorkshire Building Society.

Not far away is the 'Monday Market', half open and half housed beneath a magnificently restored Victorian cast iron and glass structure in Brook Street. This former wholesale market now shelters the general markets on Mondays and Thursdays and the Bric-a-Brac markets on Tuesdays and Saturdays that are a browsers' delight.

At the other side of the town, only five minutes walk away, is the permanent market hall. Queensgate Market with its shops and many stalls fronting onto the Piazza with the excellent Library and Art Gallery opposite. Close by is the Town Hall, home of the world famous Huddersfield Choral Society, one of the finest concert halls in the north. There are regular lunch time concerts and recitals as well as the many orchestral and choral events held in the Town Hall and other venues in the town. Two newly restored Victorian arcades, Imperial Arcade on New Street and Byram Arcade on Westgate, show different treatments of such areas.

Details of Huddersfield's many attractions and events are available from the Tourist and Information Centre, 3-5 Albion Street (0484 22133 ext 2026/2067) or the Reference Library (0484 513808 or 513803).

Huddersfield to Lockwood
(1¹/₂ miles)

After tunnelling its way out of the centre of Huddersfield, the line emerges onto a viaduct – the first of four impressive ones. This is the Longwood (or Paddock) viaduct and from it there is a panoramic view of Huddersfield. Travelling high over river and canal it is easy to picture the heavily industrialised scene of fifty years ago.

Castle Hill, on the skyline to the left, is the most striking natural landmark in the area and has been occupied since the Stone Age. The magnificent ramparts of an Iron Age hill fort were occupied by the Brigantes. These Celtic peoples dominated West Yorkshire before being defeated by the Romans in AD 71. The buildings now visible are an inn and the Jubilee Tower that was built to celebrate the 60th anniversary of Queen Victoria's reign in 1898-9. An exhibition tracing the history of the hill is on view inside the tower which is open on Bank Holidays and summer afternoons. From the top, nearly 1,000 feet above sea level, there are splendid views to all sides.

Immediately after the viaduct a short tunnel of 205 yards opens out into Lockwood station.

Castle Hill from Farnley Tyas

Lockwood to Honley
(1¼ miles)

Just beyond the station the remains of the Meltham branch line can be seen on the right. Closed in 1965, part of this line has been converted into the Healey House nature trail and picnic site by Kirklees Council.

The Lockwood viaduct is one of the largest structures of its kind in the country. At 136 feet from foundations to the top of the parapet the viaduct is beautifully constructed from the sandstone taken from cuttings excavated for the line. Fossils can still be seen in the walls of the next cutting entered soon after the viaduct.

Lockwood viaduct

7

Stone Engine – Berry Brow Station, 1904

This cutting is the site of the former Berry Brow station, with its station-master's house on the hillside to the right. All the station master's houses were built in the same style and examples can still be seen at various stations. At Berry Brow station there were the famous carvings of trains in the sandstone walls. One of these carvings was moved to the Railway Museum in York in 1963. A new station is planned to be opened at Berry Brow in 1989 nearer to Bridge Street.

Another short tunnel and Honley Station is reached. Just below this station is the Honley High School, formerly the Holme Valley Grammar School, and pupils used to be conveyed from the school up the line as far as Clayton West.

Berry Brow Station, 1904

8

Honley to Brockholes
(³/₄ mile)

The interesting village of Honley a mile away to our right is worth a visit.

A fascinating short walk around old Honley is described in the booklet *Holme Valley* by Nigel and Jenny Hinchliffe. Visit the Coach and Horses Inn where, in 1812, two members of the Luddite gang spent the night drinking after taking part in the murder of Marsden mill-owner, William Horsfall. When they were brought to trial, the landlady of the Coach and Horses went to York to give evidence. There were many sympathisers in Honley for the Luddites, whose destructiveness was born out of the desperate knowledge that the new technology meant unemployment which in turn meant nothing less than starvation.

As the railway climbs beyond Honley, the distant moors around Holme Moss appear on the right. The mast itself is 750 feet high and the moors are 1,725 feet above sea-level.

The Holme Valley along which the line runs is now nationally famous as *Last of the Summer Wine* country. A pleasant walk to Holmfirth, the *Summer Wine* town commences at Brockholes. The name Brockholes means "badger holes", and badgers can still be found in the local woodland areas.

The Coach and Horses

9

Brockholes to Stocksmoor
(2¼ miles)

The Holmfirth Branch line diverged to the right beyond Brockholes Station. Connecting the small town of Holmfirth to the railway system must have been the reason for bringing the line up this valley, as a route via Kirkburton would have been much cheaper.

The line now leaves the Holme Valley and tunnels under Thurstonland Bank. Thurstonland tunnel is, at 1631 noisy yards, the longest on the line and the fifth longest on the Lancashire and Yorkshire Railway. Apart from a short curve at the Huddersfield end it is straight.

Emerging from the tunnel the line curves into the 900 yards long Stocksmoor cutting thence into Stocksmoor station. Stocksmoor lying some distance from a main road must be one of the smallest communities still served regularly by rail. Next to the station is the Clothiers' Arms, a worthwhile destination which also welcomes children.

Brockholes Station

10

Stocksmoor to Shepley
(³/₄ mile)

Beyond Stocksmoor, Emley Moor television mast can be seen to the left. The present mast was built to replace an earlier structure that collapsed under the weight of ice in March of the very cold winter of 1969. This dominating landmark, at 1,000 feet, is higher than the Eiffel Tower.

The line now crosses a narrow wooded valley where trees disguise the height of the embankment before reaching the unusual station of Shepley with it's staggered platforms.

Shepley is an attractive village with inns, shops and very fine countryside.

Emley Moor Television Mast

The Old Woman of Stocksmoor

In January, 1864, I remember a most remarkable incident which occurred near Stocksmoor Station. I received a telegraph at Wakefield from Huddersfield in the early morning to the effect that the 9.30 p.m. passenger train from Penistone had not arrived. I at once got an engine to take me in search of it, and found the engine and train buried under a deep fall of snow, with nothing whatever to be seen but about a foot of the funnel of the engine projecting above the snow. This was in a deep cutting situated between Stocksmoor and Shepley Station. The few passengers who were in the train had been got out the previous night and taken to Shepley Station, where they remained all night.

I at once telegraphed to the permanent way inspector, at Mirfield, to bring the ballast train with some wagons and men, as the line was blocked with snow. They arrived in strong force in about an hour and a half afterwards, and commenced filling their wagons with snow and taking it away. The line was cleared and opened for traffic about midday.

In the meantime, the men requiring refreshments, I, accompanied by the locomotive inspector, went to an inn near Stocksmoor Station. On arriving at the house I saw no-one about, so went through a passage into the kitchen, and there found a woman sitting in a large old-fashioned oak chair. I asked her if she could supply a few men who were working on the railway with refreshments. She replied "Yes, I can."

Her strong voice attracted my attention. I stepped forward and stood in front of her; I took off my hat, and said, "Well, I never saw such a woman in all my life."

She then said, "When a gentleman takes off his hat to me I must rise," and she rose from her chair. I was so astonished at the size of her that I called my friend into the kitchen. When he got in he stood staring in amazement. I said "Come forward, and we will try to clasp round her," and we just managed to make the tips of our fingers meet. She then sat down in her chair, and I ordered refreshments for twenty men. Whilst the refreshments were being prepared I said I should like to know her weight. She replied:

"Ha, but I'm not going to tell you that; but you being a gentleman from t'railway, I'll tell yo' this: I wor at station t'other week, and there wor yor station master and porter, and ar policeman wer there. They all three got on to t'scale at t'weighing machine on t'platform; I put one leg on to t'other scale, when they all went up; and that's as much as i'm going to tell yo'."

However, we were quite satisfied with what was provided for us, and came away, leaving the old woman sitting comfortably in her chair.

(An extract from *The Lancashire & Yorkshire Railway*, a book published in 1898 by Thomas Normington, a native of Dewsbury, who spent almost his entire working life on the railway.)

Stocksmoor Station on the Huddersfield to Sheffield Junction Railway which opened on 1 July 1880. This photograph taken in 1910, shows some goods trucks in the sidings behind the platform while on the platform the train to Penistone is awaited.

13

Denby Dale Viaduct

Shepley to Denby Dale
(2¹/₄ miles)

The line beyond Shepley was converted to single track in 1969. A further single track conversion between Huddersfield and Stocksmoor to be done in 1989 will help to reduce operating costs. A branch line to Skelmanthorpe and Clayton West, closed as recently as 1983, can be seen on the left. This branch was built to take double track but it remained single throughout its one hundred and three years operation.

One mile after Shepley the line enters the 906 yards of the Cumberworth tunnel and a cutting, emerging in Denby Dale Station.

Denby Dale is renowned for its famous pies. The first of these was baked in 1788 to celebrate the recovery of George III from severe mental illness. Since then eight pies have been baked, the most notorious of which was the pie that went 'off' in 1887 and had to be quickly interred in a local wood.

The 1964 pie funded the building of the Pie Hall in the village and many souvenirs and photographs of the various pies are on display; the huge pie dish now stands outside the hall and is used as a flower bed! The 200th anniversary of the first Denby Dale Pie will be celebrated by the ninth pie, the largest yet, in 1988.

Denby Dale also boasts numerous shops and inns and is a fine starting point for the two walks described later in this booklet. Visitors to Denby Dale can also join the new long-distance walk following the River Dearn from its source near Birds Edge to the point near Mexborough where it joins the River Don.

A series of eight leaflets on the Dearne Way can be obtained from the Tourist Information Office in Huddersfield.

Denby Dale to Penistone
(4 miles)

Denby Dale once boasted a wooden viaduct that carried the line at a height of one hundred feet above the bed of the stream. Travellers were afraid of the wooden structure, described in a Sheffield newspaper as having a 'cobweb appearance', and it was replaced by the existing stone viaduct thirty years after the line was opened. The stone viaduct was built alongside the wooden one and the abutments can clearly be seen on the right at either end of the present viaduct that carries the line a thousand yards across the valley.

Between Denby Dale and Penistone the railway passes through delightful rural scenery with the outskirts of Barnsley barely visible in the far distance. Passing through the 415 yards of the Wellhouse tunnel and onto the last spectacular viaduct a birds eye view of Penistone can be seen. Part of the northern end of this viaduct collapsed in 1916 and an engine and two trucks crashed to the valley below! Luckily no-one was hurt.

Only a small idea can be formed nowadays of the station as it was in its heyday, when it served as the junction for four different passenger lines and the mineral line to Wath.

Penistone at 750 feet above sea level is one of the highest market towns in England. It existed before the Norman Conquest as a small village. Penistone is well worth a visit, particularly on market day, Thursday.

From here the line continues through the new station at Silkstone Common to Barnsley, with its market and shopping centre, and on to the fine city of Sheffield.

Class 142 'Pacer' at Denby Dale

The Collapse of Penistone Viaduct

Towards the end of January 1916 a slight crack had been noted in a parapet at the station end of the Penistone viaduct. Examination of the pier failed to reveal any cause for anxiety and traffic continued, with caution, while repairs were put in hand.

At seven minutes past four on the Third of February a train from Huddersfield crossed the viaduct into the station. Eight minutes later, in the course of running round the train, the engine, 2-4-2T No. 661, was standing on the track when the track was seen to be bending. The driver and fireman jumped off and ran to the station only seconds before the entire pier and two arches beneath the engine collapsed into the river. For a moment the engine remained poised on the rails and then plunged into the wreckage. After unsuccessful attempts to recover the engine whole, it had to be cut up on the spot and hauled up in sections. Some of the recovered material was used in a replacement engine built at Horwich. The cause of the collapse was stated to be scouring of the foundations after prolonged heavy rain, despite the protective works of 1883. The viaduct was repaired and re-opened on the 14 August 1916.

The chimney pot of No. 661 became a flower pot on the platform of Brockholes Station!

Collapse of Penistone Viaduct

The Scenic Route from Bradford to London

After a great deal of pressure from the Huddersfield Chamber of Commerce, an improved service of trains from Bradford and Huddersfield, via Penistone, to Sheffield and London, commenced on 1st March 1884.

On Monday, 10th March, 1884, a Bradford businessman and his companion met at the Exchange Station, Bradford, and took tickets for London, and travelled by the 1.27 p.m. train. They arrived at, and departed from, Huddersfield at the time recorded in the timetable; when the Bradford traveller said to his companion:

"Sit you there, with your face towards the engine, and just keep your eyes about you for the next half-hour or so;" and so they went, making remarks and expressions all the way, as follows:

"It was not long," says the person who tells the story, "ere I began to be so deeply interested, that I asked myself what I had been doing all these years not to have explored this region before, as we travelled through tunnellings and rocky cuttings, to veer round the edges of precipices, and dash across lofty bridges; but as you pass forward by Lockwood, Berry Brow, Honley, Brockholes, and other strangely-named places, you are taken through scenes of unsurpassing loveliness, some of them of an almost alpine character; glen after glen, and ravine after ravine are passed, with pretty manufacturing villages nestling here and there, looking far more pleasing to the eye than the villages of the worsted districts. The situation of some of the mills is picturesque in the extreme, and their surroundings are in perfect keeping. Not only are factories noticeable for their clean and neat aspect, but for their architectural beauty, which, unfortunately, is not too common a feature of this class of building. Nature has been so kind, indeed, to the dwellers in these regions, that it would have been nothing short of desecration to have erected mean-looking buildings here. As it is, the whole district seems to have been lovingly and tenderly treated by the traders who have had the building-up of its prosperity, and whichever way the eye wanders is something to be seen that appeals strongly to its sense of beauty.

Penistone Viaduct

"Is there anything on the Great Northern or the Midland (railway) to compare with this?" demanded Fred, over and over again, as we passed scene after scene of striking beauty. "Certainly not," I confessed.

"Look there!" he would cry; "What do you think of that?" as we came in sight of a tossing, foaming beck, as leaped out from the wooded hillside; and at some points we should both be seen with our heads craning out of the window, taking the fullest possible view of some spot of extraordinary charm. Presently we found ourselves rushing through Denby Dale, with an immense panorama stretching to the right and to the left, full of picturesque details; and then we came to a brief halt at Penistone, where we ran into the Manchester, Sheffield and Lincolnshire Railway line, and so forward to Sheffield, which smoke-hued town we reached about 2.50 pm."

(A further extract from Thomas Normington's book, published in 1898).

Train approaching Denby Dale Station

Travel the Penistone Line

The line from Huddersfield to Penistone offers the traveller a kaleidoscope of West Yorkshire scenery including a high level view of industrial Huddersfield, Pennine villages, rolling upland farmland and views of distant moors. The line climbs 367 feet over its relatively short length, and the view from the passenger's window between Denby Dale and Penistone cannot have altered much since it was built.

The line runs through ideal walking country; the walks listed are just a few of the many possible. The O.S. map sheet, 110 of the Landranger series and sheets SE 01/11, SE 00/10, SE 20/30, of the Pathfinder Series, cover the area, and should be considered essential for those wishing to explore it on foot. Places full of interest such as the village of Honley and the small town of Holmfirth (of *Last of the Summer Wine* fame) are within easy reach of the line. The trains continue beyond Penistone to Barnsley and Sheffield, both well worth a visit.

Plenty to see......

Plenty of interest......

Have a good trip!

Valley near Stocksmoor

21

CASTLE HILL AND FARNLEY TYAS WALK

Castle Hill and Farnley Tyas Walk
(5 miles)

This is an interesting walk amid contrasting scenery with glorious views of the moors towards Holme Moss.

From Honley station, turn right towards G.B. Hirst's fence, and go through the snicket on the left. Turn right onto the road for 30 yards then take the footpath ahead. When the road bends to the right, continue up through the fields to the road at the top. Cross diagonally right to the opposite stile and go through this field until you reach a stile in the wall on your left. Continue with the wall now to your right, through a stile in the facing wall, skirt the wood, pass through a gateway and go forward with a wall to your left to the next gateway. Turn left and cross the end of a green lane at the next facing wall, continuing forward to another. Cross this and turn right at the second of the two stiles to go forward until the road is reached. Here turn left to the top, where some steps on the right lead you onto Castle Hill, where you will want to spend some time. The tower is open at weekends during the summer and Bank Holidays.

From here you can retrace your steps or return via the road to Honley station. To continue the walk, go down the metalled road from the public house and after the first sharp bend double back on a narrow path between the bushes. Continue down through a field to cross a farm road. Go steeply down a field to join a road at the bottom, here turn right and just before a farm turn left into fields. (If you emerge onto the road between the houses at Lumb turn left until you reach the stile into the fields). You are aiming for Farnley Tyas whose church spire can be seen ahead. Follow a well-beaten path down to a stream and up through woods, fields and lane to the village. Turn right past the Golden Cock. Take the right hand road at the fork to the first stile on the left. Follow through Hey Wood to Honley station.

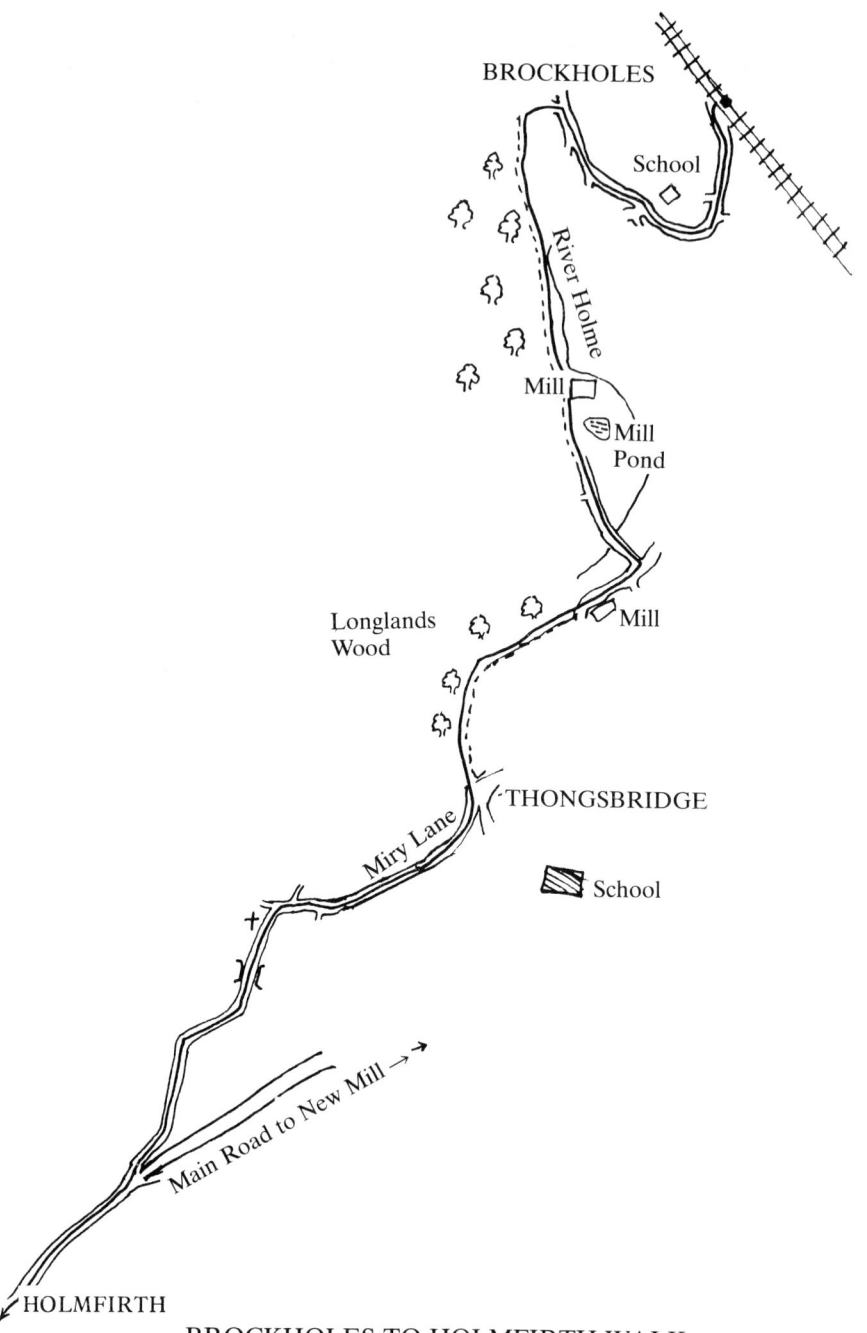

BROCKHOLES

School

River Holme

Mill

Mill
Pond

Longlands
Wood

Mill

THONGSBRIDGE

Miry Lane

School

Main Road to New Mill →

HOLMFIRTH

BROCKHOLES TO HOLMFIRTH WALK

24

Brockholes to Holmfirth Walk
(2 miles)

For those wanting to walk to Holmfirth, here is a pleasant and easy walk, fairly dry underfoot.

Go down the lane from Brockholes station to the village, bearing right along Brockholes Lane. At the main road turn right, and then first road left over a humpbacked bridge into Smith Place Lane. Look left after about 100 yards for a public footpath sign by a telegraph post, go through the gate and yard to the clearly defined path beyond. (Should you miss this, take the stone steps up the bank a little further on.) Continue through the woods, keeping the river on your left. When you come out into a lane turn right, and then left in front of some buildings to reach a metalled road after crossing the river by a footbridge.

Norah Batty's house!

Turn right onto the road, and at the first sharp bend left, turn right up some steps alongside a mill. Continue along the path, keeping the wall to your left until a road is reached. Go forward down the hill and turn left up a narrow lane just before the church. After crossing a bridge that has been filled in, take the right fork. Follow this lane until it joins the main road at Holmfirth. Go down the hill to the town centre.

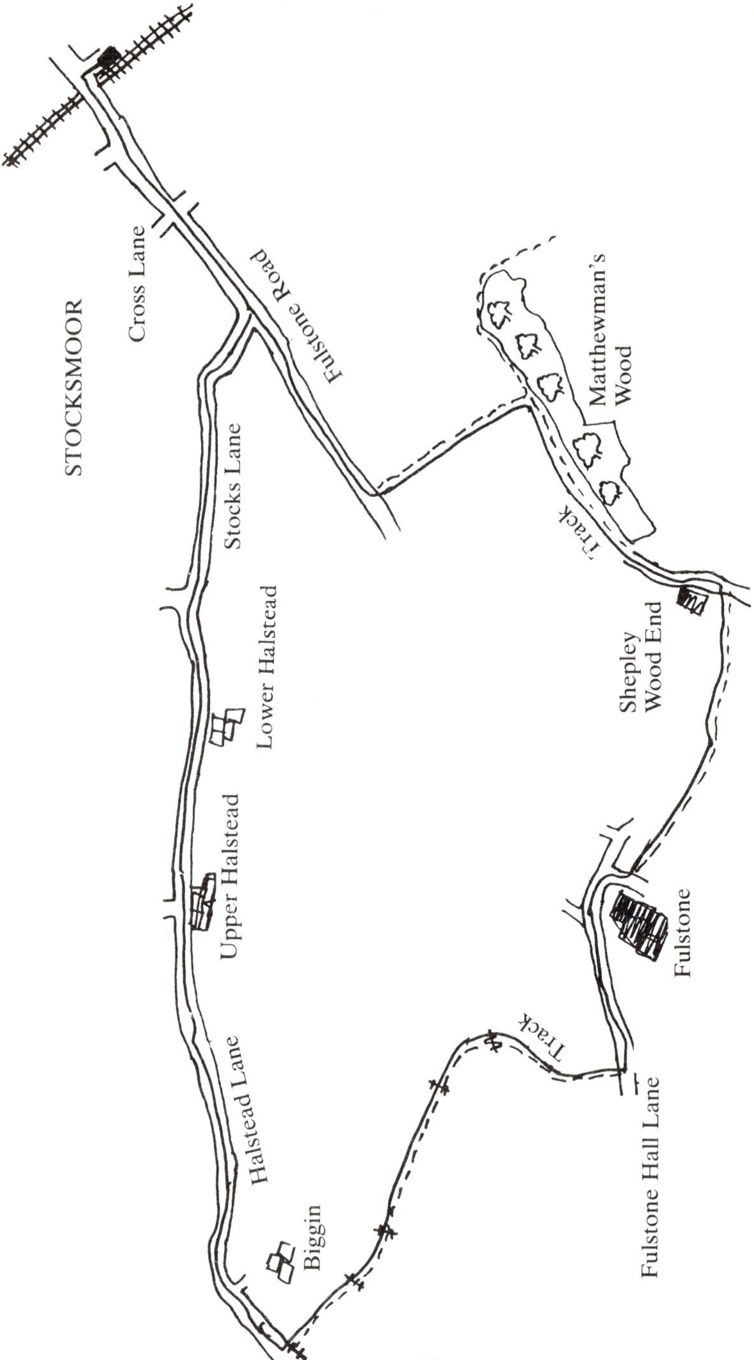

STOCKSMOOR

Cross Lane

Fulstone Road

Stocks Lane

Lower Halstead

Upper Halstead

Halstead Lane

Biggin

Matthewman's Wood

Track

Shepley Wood End

Fulstone

Track

Fulstone Hall Lane

STOCKSMOOR CIRCULAR WALK

Stocksmoor Circular Walk
(5 miles)

On leaving Stocksmoor station turn left onto the lane, straight ahead at the crossroads and then right onto Stocks Lane and then Halstead Lane.

Follow this quiet lane for some distance, past Lower Halstead, Upper Halstead and Biggin. There are magnificent views of the Holme Valley and Fulstone village on its hill over to the left to be admired.

As the lane drops down, past Biggin on the left and New Biggin on the right, a signpost indicates a footpath into a field on the left. Follow the path across the fields (using the stiles as a guide) toward Fulstone.

The path eventually emerges onto the lane below Fulstone. Walk uphill, right at the junction and then immediately left at a footpath sign onto a narrow track between a garden and a field.

Follow the path across the fields up the hill towards the top corner of the wood. The path emerges through a gate onto a track at the right-hand side of the farm buildings ahead. Turn left onto the track through the farm and beyond it, heading across the fields towards Stocksmoor.

The next turn is hard to spot. Five or six hundred yards after the farm you must turn left and walk down across the fields to the wooded valley bottom. The path originally went alongside a stone wall which is now gone but a gateway helps mark the spot.

In the woods below a flight of stone steps leads down to the stream. Cross the stream and turn right onto the country lane which leads back to Stocksmoor.

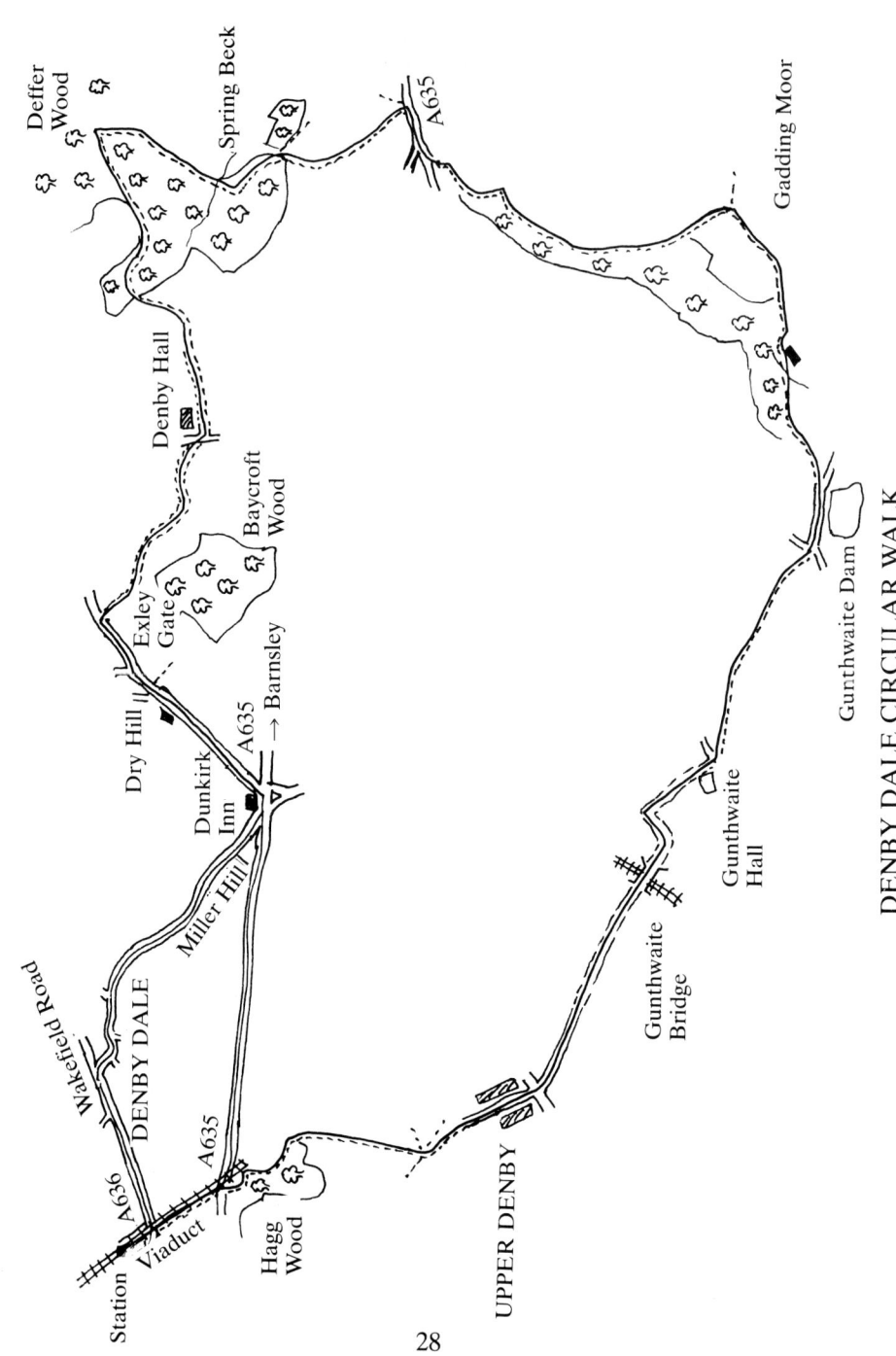

DENBY DALE CIRCULAR WALK

Denby Dale Circular Walk
(7 miles)

From the station, go down through the works yard and approach road to the A636. Go under the bridge and down the steps on the left to walk alongside the viaduct. Cross the A635 and take the path opposite to follow the well marked track to Upper Denby. Keep to the top road through the village and you will reach the B6115 opposite Gunthwaite Lane. Follow the lane for a mile until it becomes a bridle path at the second sharp left turn by Gunthwaite Hall. Continue down this clearly marked path, and when it emerges onto a metalled road go forward with the stretch of water to your right.

Shortly after the road leaves the water turn left along the track to Mill Farm, where you will cross the stream. Head up the far bank and veer left to a stile over the wall. Follow the path through the fields to reach a green lane by a stile and gate (and footpath sign), at the corner of a belt of trees. Turn left onto this bridleway and follow it through the woods for half a mile until you come out onto a road where you turn right and cross the stream. Go forward as you join the A635, keeping the stream to your right, and after a few yards take the stile on the left up a path with a hedge to your right. As two woods come into sight make for the gap between them, keeping the hedge to your right.

Where the hedge gives place to a stone wall, turn left across the field and enter the higher wood. Follow the path up through the wood, keeping fields to your right. Soon after the path turns into the wood turn left at a public footpath sign. (It is possible to come out at a footpath sign slightly higher up the wood than this one, but do not worry, turn left at this, and when shortly after you meet the other sign, keep right). Eventually you will find a field to your right again. Keep going forward, enter a neck of the wood, and where the wood ends continue across the fields to a farm. This is Denby Hall Farm, approach it with the main farm buildings to your right. Turn right on the lane to pass in front of the farm. Here turn left and go across the fields. Keeping the wood ahead to your left, aim for its top edge, and then with a wall on your left head for a pylon by a metalled road.

Turn left at the road and take the next lane to the right, then take the first lane to the left. After half a mile Denby Dale will come into sight; you have a choice of routes back to the station at the far end of the village.

29

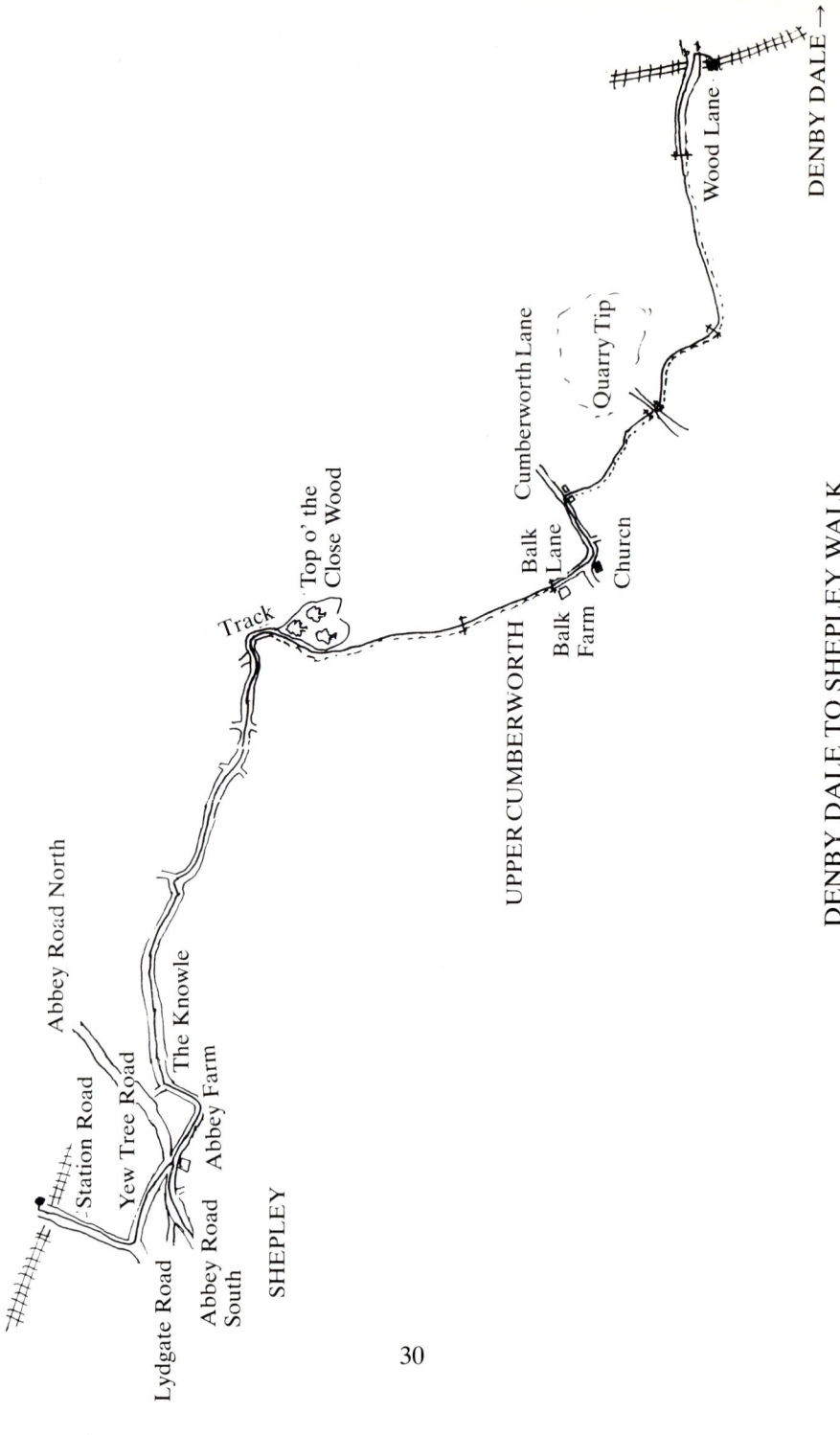

DENBY DALE →

Wood Lane

Quarry Tip

Cumberworth Lane

Top o' the
Close Wood

Track

UPPER CUMBERWORTH

Balk
Lane

Church

Balk
Farm

Abbey Road North

Station Road

Yew Tree Road

The Knowle

Abbey Farm

Lydgate Road

Abbey Road
South

SHEPLEY

DENBY DALE TO SHEPLEY WALK

Denby Dale to Shepley Walk
(4 miles)

Leave the station through the builder's yard and turn left onto the bridge which crosses the line. Take the left fork onto the track, over a wooden stile and into the field ahead. From here fine views unfold; of Denby Dale viaduct (behind and left), over towards High Flatts (ahead and left) and of Cumberworth Church (ahead and right).

Leave the large field over a stile at the right-hand corner and turn right onto a narrow track alongside the Council tip. This track soon emerges by a "Public Footpath" sign onto the slip road to the tip.

After 100 yards (past a redundant stile) turn left over another stone stile and, immediately after entering the next field turn right and walk straight ahead until the path emerges between the last two houses onto Cumberworth Lane.

Turn left and, just before the church, right onto Balk Lane, over a stone stile and into the fields ahead. From here the land drops down towards Shepley. Walk straight ahead across the fields, through a small woodland and onto an unmade lane.

Follow the lane round to the left, across a country road, along a clearly marked track which veers left into Knowle Road, Shepley. Follow this street round until it emerges into the main Huddersfield to Sheffield road.

You can now either turn right down to the station or left into Shepley village, with buses to Huddersfield, Penistone, Holmfirth or Denby Dale and Wakefield.

Acknowledgements

LESLEY BROOK for maps (based on Ordnance Survey, Crown Copyright reserved) on pages 22, 24, 26, 28, 30.

JENNY HINCHLIFFE for illustrations on pages iii, 9, 25.

HUDDERSFIELD EXAMINER for photograph on page 20.

HUDDERSFIELD LOCAL STUDIES LIBRARY for photographs on pages 4, 8, 10, 13.

DAVID THURLOW for photographs and illustrations on cover and pages i, 2, 3, 4, 6, 7, 11, 14, 16, 17, 19, 21.